EXPLORING WORSHIP

BOB SORGE

Workbook & Discussion Guide

OASIS HOUSE
KANSAS CITY, MISSOURI

Exploring Worship: Workbook & Discussion Guide

Published by Oasis House
PO Box 522
Grandview, MO 64030-0522
816-767-8880

International Standard Book Number: 978-1-937725-63-1

Stay connected with us at:
YouTube.com/bobsorge
Instagram: bob.sorge
Store: oasishouse.com
Blog: bobsorge.com
Twitter.com/BOBSORGE
Facebook.com/BobSorgeMinistry

For more on Bob's books, go to page 48.

CONTENTS

EXPLORING WORSHIP

WORKBOOK & DISCUSSION GUIDE

INSTRUCTIONS

1. Read a chapter in *EXPLORING WORSHIP.*
2. Then complete that chapter in this Workbook. As you do, you'll automatically revisit the major ideas in that chapter.
3. For confirmation, the answers are provided in the back of this Workbook.
4. FOR GROUP DISCUSSION: When your group gathers, go through these discussion questions together.
5. EXPLORING DEEPER: These questions are for individual study. They'll guide you as you dig deeper into the content of each chapter.

This Workbook is written for:

- Classrooms: *EXPLORING WORSHIP* is one of the leading tools available for training worship students. This Workbook facilitates classroom discussion, strengthens content retention, monitors student participation, and promotes deeper engagement.
- Local churches: Take your entire worship ministry through the Book and Workbook together! If you do, your team is sure to grow in vision, unity, understanding, and depth.
- Bible Study Groups: *EXPLORING WORSHIP* is an excellent study for small groups in praise and worship. Together, the Book and Workbook comprise a unique manual for educating, inspiring, training, and mobilizing worshipers in these last days.

CHAPTER ONE

WHAT IS PRAISE?

1. Some dictionary definitions given for praise: ______________________

____

____

____

2. An American idiom for praise: ______________________

3. The Bible shows us that praise is to be declared or ______________________.

4. We don't praise God our own personal way, we praise ______________________ way.

5. What do we praise? List four things. ______________________

____

____

6. Every name of God reveals something about ______________________

____

7. Give six reasons why we should praise the Lord.

   1. ______________________
   2. ______________________
   3. ______________________
   4. ______________________
   5. ______________________
   6. ______________________

8. It's not that He needs our praises, but He knows ______________________________

____.

9. Write out the Shorter Catechism. ______________________________

____

10. List four times when we should praise the Lord. ______________________________

____

11. While praise is not emotionalism, it is ______________________.

12. List three places where we should praise the Lord. ______________________________

____

____

13. Write out one of the verses that says we should praise God in the congregation.

____

____

14. Give three reasons why lifting our hands is meaningful. ______________________________

____

____

____

15. List ten ways to praise the Lord. ______________________________

____

____

____

16. The idea of hand clapping in Scripture doesn't seem to be so much a keeping of the beat as it is ____.

17. What piece of furniture seemed to be absent from the tabernacle? ____________

18. Give two functions that standing serves in praise. ____________

____

____

19. What's the most common posture of worship in the Book of Revelation? ____________

____

20. I wonder if we resist dancing before the Lord because ____________

____________.

21. When we initiate a physical release, it's often followed by a ____________

____________.

22. Dancing is a biblical way to love the Lord with your ____________.

23. What reason did the brother in Spain give for why we dance? ____________

____

____

____

24. It's a sad day for the church when ____________

____________ is no longer heard in the camp.

FOR GROUP DISCUSSION

1. Choose a couple fill-in-the-blank statements above to talk about in the group.
2. Look at the four things listed in the WHAT DO WE PRAISE section. Are those four complete, or should we add a fifth to the list? When we keep those four before us, how can they help us be more spontaneous in praise?
3. Ten ways to praise the Lord are listed. The last three are probably the most controversial. Why are they controversial? How should they be expressed? Are they appropriate to be expressed in our church? Which of the ten is most meaningful to you personally?

EXPLORING DEEPER

1. Do an online search, and write out some definitions of praise that you find. Can you find a verse to support each definition?
2. Can you identify any other scriptural ways to praise the Lord that are not specifically mentioned in this chapter?
3. In the King James Version, seven Hebrew words are translated "praise" in English. Look up the Hebrew words that your Bible translates "praise," and write down what you learn about each Hebrew word.
4. Compile a list of the names of God in Scripture, and then take time to worship Him for the attributes of each name.

NOTES

CHAPTER TWO

ENTERING THE PRESENCE OF GOD

1. Describe the three varying manifestations of the presence of God.

   1. ____________________

   2. ____________________

   3. ____________________

2. Like those priests of old, we want to be so taken with God that He is ____________________ ____________________.

3. There's no universal ____________________ for entering God's presence.

4. Write out a verse that says we enter His presence with praise. ____________________

5. Write out a verse that says we enter His presence with worship. ____________________

6. Our primary posture in worship is not that of receiving but ____________________.

7. The first and foremost responsibility of every worship is to ____________________ ____________________.

8. If something has distanced us from the Lord, what should we do? ____________________

____

____

9. When we invest prayer for the worship service, our ______________________________

____ go to another level.

10. When a congregation gathers to worship, they're making a statement before what three things? ____

____

____

11. Come with a ____________________ offering, and also come with an offering of the ______________________________________.

12. Corporate praise is not automatically glorious. We must ____________ it glorious.

13. As worshipers, we don't want to be like that ____________, waiting for the worship leader to scratch us in just the right place so we can ______________________.

14. When Jesus called His disciples "slow of heart" (Luke 24:25), it wasn't exactly ____________________.

15. Resolve to push aside __________________ when coming into the Lord's presence.

16. We have a responsibility to be worshipers all ____________________ long.

17. Sometimes, if praise is to happen, it requires a selfless _____________ on our part.

18. What do you do when your soul is downcast? You offer up ____________________

____.

19. God delights in the sacrifices of a ____________________ heart.

20. It's not a sacrifice until it ____________________ something.

21. That's precisely the time, however, when we have opportunity to offer up a __________

____

and bless the Lord with our heart, soul, mind, and strength.

22. Just as it takes more than five _______________ to have a meaningful interaction with a friend or spouse, fulfilling communion with Jesus will cost us ____________.

FOR GROUP DISCUSSION

1. Choose a couple fill-in-the-blank statements above to talk about in the group.
2. Talk about the analogy in this chapter of putting on spiritual makeup. What does that metaphor mean to you? How have you intentionally prepared yourself for worship?
3. During corporate worship, are you tempted to get into discernment mode and start analyzing what's going on in the meeting? What's your strongest temptation in this regard? How do you put these kinds of distractions behind you?
4. The author wrote, "The goal of worship leaders, therefore, is not simply to cultivate thirty minutes of exuberant worship on Sunday mornings but to cultivate worshipers who live a life of praise all week long." How can we do that?
5. Discuss your church's typical format in praise and worship. What are the strengths of your church's format? Do you perceive any accompanying weaknesses? Are there any ways we can grow and continue to move forward together?
6. Have you ever been frustrated with people who are not self-motivated to praise the Lord? How have you learned to deal with that frustration?

EXPLORING DEEPER

1. Study the many effects the presence of God has had upon people in the Bible. Which stories inspire you the most? What can we learn from them?
2. Research the Scriptures for further insight into the differences between individual and corporate worship.
3. What connections can you discover between the Old Testament sacrifices and the New Testament "sacrifice of praise?"

NOTES

CHAPTER THREE

PRAISE: A WEAPON FOR SPIRITUAL WARFARE

1. The second paragraph mentions five means through which spiritual victories are won. List them. ______________________________

____

____

2. Corporate worship is an assault on the ______________ of ______________.

3. Moses and all Israel sang a triumphal song of victory before the Lord and celebrated with this declaration: "The LORD is a ______________ of ______________: the LORD is his name" (Exod 15:3).

4. He's also the ______________ of heaven's hosts.

5. "We don't need to fight. We just need to stand and watch the salvation of God. Well, since that's the case, let's ______________ the ______________!"

6. He made the choir the ______________.

7. Off they went to war, with the choir ______________ and the army ______________.

8. The real warriors on that occasion were not the ______________ in the army but the ______________ in the choir.

9. They weren't telling God ______________ to defeat the enemy, they were just praising Him because they knew He ______________.

10. Midnight is a good time for ________________ to sing praises to God!
11. They were advertising the ________________ of God in a context where no one could see any of His ________________.
12. They didn't rebuke the ________________ or curse the _. They simply praised God for His ________________ and goodness.
13. Not only were Paul and Silas freed from their ________________, but an entire family was ________________ from the clutches of Satan.
14. The people of Israel used a ________________ of ________________ to overcome the city of Jericho.
15. In response to their ________________, the Lord fought for Israel. He caused the Midianite army to ________________ and kill one another.
16. It's a sad day for the church when the ________________ is gone from the camp.
17. When we ________________ in His strength, He goes to ________________. We ________________; He ________________.
18. How can He do anything but respond to such simple, bold ________________?
19. We don't pretend to have ________________ over the enemy in ourselves, but we do ________________ in the God who does.
20. Young children are utterly ________________ when it comes to fighting battles the world's way, but they are ________________ enough to lift their voices in ________________ to the God who fights for them.
21. What is the twofold combination God has given us in Psalm 149 to defeat our enemies?

____

____

22. What are five possible meanings of "high praise?" ____________________

____

____

____

23. There is a beautiful relationship between the singing of God's __ and the preaching and singing of the ____________________.

24. After their ____________________ praise, Peter's sermon cut like a ____________________ sword, and about three thousand people repented and came to Christ.

25. When the time is right, the Lord will empower a ____________________ ministry to lead the ____________________ in high praise.

26. To your intercessions add ____________________.

27. We go to war through praise only through the specific ____________________ of the Holy Spirit.

28. A worship ministry might gather on Saturday night and ____________________ together on behalf of the next day's service.

29. Sometimes we don't find a full ____________________ in corporate worship because we ____________________ too soon.

FOR GROUP DISCUSSION

1. Choose a couple fill-in-the-blank statements above to talk about in the group.
2. Do you have a story about spiritual warfare to share with the group?
3. Do you use praise on a repeated basis to bring spiritual release in your life? How has God honored your faith?

4. Did Jesus finish the battle on the cross, or do we still engage in spiritual battles today? How do we reconcile the finished work of the cross with the intensity of today's warfare?
5. How can we be more intentional in using praise in spiritual warfare in our church?
6. What's the relationship between praise in spiritual warfare, and faith?

EXPLORING DEEPER

1. Study the scriptural truth that God fights for us. How is this truth expressed in New Testament terms?
2. Do a word study on the Hebrew words that are translated "shout," and see their connection with praise. How common was the practice of shouting in the praise of the Hebrews?
3. Using Psalm 144:1 as a springboard, can you find other indications in the Bible that God encourages us to apply ourselves with diligence to the mastering of our musical instruments and vocal abilities?

NOTES

CHAPTER FOUR

WHAT IS WORSHIP?

1. Of those listed, write out the three definitions for worship that you affirm the most.

____

____

____

____

2. Worship is not a ______________ activity but an expression of the ______________.
3. God doesn't need our ______________, but He does seek ______________.
4. We ______________ ourselves so we can ______________ Him.
5. Notice that God seeks ______________, not worship.
6. Praise can function like a ______________ street, but worship is ______________ communion and fellowship.
7. Praise is always seen or ______, but worship isn't always ________ to an observer.
8. Praise is very aware of other ______________ in the room. In worship, however, we lose sight of ________ around us and become preoccupied with the wonder of who He is.
9. Praise often acts as a ______________ to worship
10. Speaking to ______________ in song is biblical.
11. Worship is what we do in the face of great ______________ and personal ______________.

12. The test of worship doesn't happen on ____________________ morning.

    It happens on ____________________ morning.

13. The ____________________ line on worship is loving the Lord in the midst of our greatest ____________________.

14. For Abraham, worship meant putting on the altar all his hopes, ____________________, aspirations, and ____________________. It meant giving God his ____________________.

15. Worship is an expression of ____________________. Therefore, worship is ____________________.

16. Worship is the ____________________ within us calling out to the ____________________ in God.

17. Worship is staring at ____________________.

18. It takes ____________________ to love God.

19. In corporate worship gatherings, the Holy Spirit is our ____________________.

20. A meeting is not ____________________ if we've merely followed our set list; it's successful if we've followed the ____________________.

21. Not only does the Holy Spirit ____________________ to lead our times of corporate worship, He's really ____________________ at it.

22. The best way a worship team can help people ____________________ with God is by connecting with God ____________________.

23. True worship is experienced at the height of ____________________ awareness.

24. To *worship in truth* doesn't mean we must be ____________________; it just means we're not hiding anything or making ____________________.

25. When you worship in truth, truth becomes ____________________ in you.

26. The psalmist anointing wasn't primarily a ____________________ anointing but a ____________________ anointing.

27. May we discover David's secret of using theas a catalyst for worship.

28. For your heart to ______________ in worship, it must be grounded in ____________.

29. The deeper you go in ______________________, the higher you can soar in the ______________________.

30. Increased levels of exertion can turn into ______________________.

31. The Holy Spirit is profoundly committed to keeping the first ______________________ in first ______________________ in our lives.

32. We'll be ______________ who work rather than workers who ________________.

33. There's only one thing that's really necessary, and that is to ______________________ lovingly at Jesus' feet and ______________________ His words.

FOR GROUP DISCUSSION

1. Choose a couple fill-in-the-blank statements above to talk about in the group.
2. Have you heard people debate about whether praise and worship should be horizontal or vertical? If both are valid, what are their roles?
3. Has the Lord taught you how to love Him even when suffering? What have you learned about worshiping in a trial?
4. Worship in Spirit and in truth—what does that mean to you?

EXPLORING DEEPER

1. Identify three Scriptures that especially help you connect with Jesus at the heart level in worship. Write them in a place where your eye will catch them daily.
2. Study the role of the Holy Spirit as our Worship Leader. Which verses stand out to you?
3. Continue to study what it means to worship in Spirit and in truth. and journal your insights.
4. Ask the Lord to show you how to maintain your first love.

NOTES

CHAPTER FIVE

BECOMING A WORSHIPER

1. By pouring this oil on Jesus, she was making a ____________________ sacrifice.
2. In bringing this ____________________ to Jesus, she realized there was no way to give only part; it was all or ____________________.
3. Will we waste our lives on ourselves or ____________________?
4. They were not to appear before God without a ____________________.
5. The dignity and honor of giving to the Lord from the strength of our labors should be ____________________ designed as an integral part of worship.
6. The ____________________ and poured oil reflected her wholehearted repentance.
7. Never relent until you ____________________ while meditating in the word of God.
8. The Greek word for worship—*proskuneo*—means *to kiss the* ____________________ *toward.*
9. But ____________________ is sometimes part of the cost of being a true worshiper.
10. Love is not bound by protocol or ____________________.
11. She despised the thought that a king would behave in such an ____________________ manner.
12. If we become critical of genuine acts of worship, we could hazard spiritual ____________________.
13. Jesus never despises ____________________ affection.
14. Worship is more than a theology; it's an effusion of ____________________.
15. The elders around the throne are among the foremost of heaven's ____________________ of worship before the Lamb.

16. May I never become so mature as a believer that I lose my enthusiasm and ______________________ for the fame of His name!

17. When we give our hearts to the Lord in extravagant worship, we carry with us the ______________________ of Christ.

18. First she worshiped; ______________________ she was forgiven.

19. We don't have to be ______________________ before we draw near to Him.

20. The accuser wants us to feel so unworthy that we ______________________ God's presence.

21. As we worship in intimacy we gain strength to ______________________ sin.

22. Conviction leads to ______________________; condemnation leads to ______________________.

23. The glory of His presence affects our sinfulness like ______________________ affects cancer.

24. The only time it's inappropriate to worship God with sin in your life is when you have no intention of ______________________.

25. ______________________ has ruined more worship services than all the forces of hell combined.

26. ______________________ fails to honor God's holiness, and supposes we can approach Him in our own way and on our own terms.

27. But the biblical paradigm for corporate worship was never anything close to a ______________________ model.

28. Are we simply ______________________ to the music without really being gripped by the message of the song?

29. Music is a ____________________, not an end in itself.

30. Even if the worship leader is ________________________ or self-proclaiming, God is still worthy of my praise.

FOR GROUP DISCUSSION

1. Choose a couple fill-in-the-blank statements above to talk about in the group.
2. As you've matured as a worshiper, have you found giving to take on a new meaning for you? How?
3. What are some ways we can become more authentic and wholehearted in our worship?
4. Are tears a meaningful expression for you in worship?
5. How have you personally learned to overcome accusation from the accuser and your conscience?
6. Of the "Other Hindrances" listed at the end of the chapter, which one hinders you most?

EXPLORING DEEPER

1. Worshipers carry the fragrance of Christ. Can you see this truth in the burning of incense in Moses' tabernacle, or in any other portions of Scripture?
2. Do a study in the Book of Romans on the righteousness of God that is given to us by grace through faith.
3. What is the redemptive role of tears in Scripture?
4. What aspects of the cross make your worship even more wholehearted?

NOTES

CHAPTER SIX

THE PURPOSE OF CONGREGATIONAL WORSHIP

1. Each church must determine for themselves what ______________ they desire worship to fulfill in the life of the local church.
2. In this model, corporate singing is viewed as a way to ______________ the presence of God.
3. The smartest thing we can do is ______________ in worship upon the Lord.
4. In a day when the world blasphemes and curses Him, we lift our hands high and tell Him how ______________ He is.
5. The cry of the worshiper is not, "Bless me, Lord," but rather, "Bless the ______________, O my soul!"
6. By blessing the Lord we're automatically ______________.
7. The worship service provides a glorious opportunity to forget about ______________ and get taken up with God.
8. The purpose of the worship team is to ______________, not divert, the way worshipers engage with the Lord.
9. Sometimes we need to intentionally turn off our ______________ and take up our holy calling of ministering to the Lord.
10. We can bring Him the blessing and praise of an ______________ heart.
11. We worship in order to experience the ______________ of God.

12. The presence of God is the ______________________ of the church.
13. Where worship is absent, ______________________ will also be absent.
14. A worship service will provide an atmosphere that is conducive to the ______________________ of the gifts of the Spirit.
15. We worship to open up the channels of ______________________ between us and God.
16. He longs for us to lower our guard, lift our ______________________, and give expression to our love in His presence.
17. It's fantastic to connect vertically with Jesus; but it's also wonderful to connect ______________________ with other believers.
18. Praise and worship are holy catalysts designed by the Lord to ______________________ and express our unity.
19. When you pray and praise with someone, your heart is ______________________ to that person.
20. We literally ______________________ one another.
21. We praise in order to ______________________ and reinforce spiritual truth.
22. Singing Scripture is an amazingly effective way to help our ______________________ memorize and learn the Scriptures.
23. Praise provides believers with an opportunity to ______________________ their faith before others.
24. God never intended His praises be confined to the ears of ______________________.
25. Praise is God's ______________________ campaign.
26. Praise and worship foster ______________________ for the word.

27. Worship frees the ______________________.

28. Worship increases our ______________________.

29. Worship ______________________ us into the image of Christ.

30. Worship softens our hearts and helps us keep ______________________ with the new things God wants to do.

FOR GROUP DISCUSSION

1. Choose a couple fill-in-the-blank statements above to talk about in the group.
2. What do you consider to be the main purposes of worship in your church? Which purposes in this chapter don't really apply to your church? How would you articulate your vision for worship in your church?
3. Discuss the horizontal dynamics of praise in your church. Does your church function in a healthy way in these aspects?
4. Worship is vertical, horizontal, and inward. Which of these does your church need to develop more?

EXPLORING DEEPER

1. Beginning with Song of Solomon 2:14, compile a set of Scriptures in which God urges us to open our hearts and lives to him without reservation.
2. Find scriptural support for the statement, "praise increases our faith."
3. Starting with Isaiah 6:1-7, research the thread throughout Scripture that reinforces the idea that worship is seeing the Lord.

NOTES

CHAPTER SEVEN

MOVING PROPHETICALLY IN PRAISE AND WORSHIP

1. When a spirit of worship takes over a room we could also call it a spirit of ____________________ .

2. Write out the author's definition: *To move prophetically in worship is to* ____

3. In some services, we need a kingdom ____________________ from the Lord to unlock what the Spirit wants to do.

4. Worship is an ____________________ or dialogue—it's two-way communication.

5. He loves us first, and then He ____________________ us to love Him back.

6. Worship's potential is unlocked when we value the relationship between ____________________ (us speaking) and ____________________ (God speaking).

7. They sang prophecies, and they also ____________________ upon their instruments.

8. I've been in services where a drummer played an unexpected drum solo in such a Spirit-inspired way that it ____________________ the meeting open.

9. The musician used his gift to release Elisha's ________________ anointing.
10. He was both musician and ________________.
11. If God has called someone to a music ministry, He has also ________________ that person to function prophetically.
12. A prophetic spirit might come upon a singer and they might begin to sing a song as though ________________ were singing back to His bride.
13. By *psalms*, Paul meant the singing of ________________.
14. He was referring to songs of ________________ composition.
15. By *spiritual songs,* Paul was referring to spontaneous songs of the ________________.
16. Hymns that have survived the centuries tend to be exceptionally ________________ in content.
17. Resurrecting old songs by giving them a musical ________________ helps to keep us connected to our heritage of faith.
18. In recent years, spiritual songs have been taking the entire body of Christ by ________________.
19. We don't always have to sing ________________ songs in order to experience authentic worship.
20. It's possible for an individual to sing a spiritual song that benefits and ________________ the entire congregation.
21. If a public expression of praise produces a stronger level of praise in the ________________ congregation, then we consider it profitable.
22. When we testify about Jesus in song, our singing is probably under a ________________ of prophecy.

23. He also desired for me to sing spiritual songs and have __________ in singing prophetic songs.
24. Prophetic utterances are unlocked by __________.
25. Growth requires boldness to make mistakes and __________.
26. That's what prophetic song is all about–giving Jesus opportunity to __________ over His people.
27. Spiritual songs spring from the reality of a fiery __________ with Jesus.
28. A valid utterance edifies the entire congregation, so it must be __________ by all.

FOR GROUP DISCUSSION

1. Choose a couple fill-in-the-blank statements above to talk about in the group.
2. Review the definition at the beginning of the chapter on moving prophetically in worship. Is that definition helpful and relevant for your church?
3. What are practical ways our church can flow prophetically in worship?
4. Discuss the author's respective definitions of psalms, hymns, and spiritual songs (as Paul uses the terms in Ephesians 5:19). Does our church have a healthy balance of all three?

EXPLORING DEEPER

1. Study the role of faith as it relates to the unlocking of the prophetic gifting. Start with Romans 12:6.
2. Based upon your knowledge of the Scriptures and your own personal experience, add your own suggestions to the guidelines of things to do and avoid when expressing the prophetic gifting.
3. What do the Scriptures reveal about God singing?

NOTES

CHAPTER EIGHT

THE ART OF LEADING WORSHIP

1. Congregational singing requires that a worship leader be ____________________.
2. True worshipers worship whether they're ____________________ or not.
3. We don't want a spiritual ____________________ leading our worship services.
4. The leader must be musically inclined to a level that is ____________________ for that specific church.
5. A leader should feel ____________________ with the church's theology, doctrine, and government.
6. Let the greatness of the calling ____________________ you to walk more closely with God.
7. Rhythmic stability is helpful in worship, which is why ____________________ are helping so many worship teams.
8. Drummers should also develop the skill of changing the ____________________ of a song mid-song.
9. Every song a worship team masters becomes another ____________________ at their disposal.
10. Ride a wave all the way to the ____________________.
11. Just as a plant can be harmed by too much water, a worship service can get ____________________ down by too many songs.
12. Be prepared to help ____________________ understand some of the ways we worship.

13. They're not inspired by your attainments but by your ______________.

14. Worship leading is taking your private cry and making it ______________.

15. Leaders who maintain this kind of high platform profile can actually ______________ people from worship.

16. The onus comes on the entire worship team to strive for the maximum degree of ______________ possible.

17. Worship leaders are ______________ of worship.

18. The goal of the worship leader is to provide the best ______________ possible for the people to worship.

19. Almost every worship leader has to grapple at some point with the propensity to ______________ in human energy.

20. ______________ control, then ______________ control.

21. When we surrender our control, we open to the ______________ of a Spirit-led worship service.

22. A one-sentence exhortation at the right moment can make a ______________ in a meeting.

23. With every exhortation, be sensitive to those in a ______________ season of life.

24. If you do exhort, say it as ______________ as you can.

25. Sometimes He'll deliberately engineer a ______________ worship service.

26. You can't always tell by the expressions on people's faces whether they're ______________ with God.

27. I prefer a church ______________ in which worshipers are not told every move to make.

28. Somebody once described a rut as a ____________________ with the ends knocked out.

29. I recommend adopting goals for corporate worship that are so clear they are actually ____________________ down.

30. We're not laboring merely for 20 hot minutes on a Sunday morning; we're laboring to develop ____________________ who worship Jesus in a 24/7 reality.

FOR GROUP DISCUSSION

1. Choose a couple fill-in-the-blank statements above to talk about in the group.
2. Have you seen the tendency of some to "worship worship"? How can we avoid this pitfall?
3. Talk about the dictum, Get control then lose control. How does that help us lead worship more effectively?
4. In what way is the metaphor of surfing similar to what happens in corporate worship?
5. Talk about some of the ruts your church's worship tends to fall into. How can we get out of the ruts?

EXPLORING DEEPER

1. Gather your own list of Scriptures that are good springboards for exhortation when encouraging the saints to praise.
2. Interview a number of pastors and church leaders and come up with some creative solutions to two problems in congregational worship: making the offering a meaningful expression of worship, and; incorporating standing in worship without tiring the weak.
3. Read a book on church leadership and apply the principles to worship leading.

NOTES

CHAPTER NINE

THE WORSHIP TEAM

1. We're not simply trying to get a bonfire going on the platform; we're seeking to start a ____________________ in the congregation.
2. The worship team breaks open a ____________________ in music and song so that the congregation can follow.
3. The first benefit of team ministry, therefore, is ____________________.
4. When a vision is communicated clearly, and a team gathers prayerfully around that vision, the kingdom of God ____________________ dynamically in a region.
5. No one can mobilize and ____________________ the worship team more effectively than the pastor.
6. Who better to teach the team how to ____________________?
7. Pastors are key to the worship ministry in their role as lead ____________________.
8. The pastors' demeanor can do more to influence the ____________________ of the congregation than the efforts of the musicians, singers, and worship leader combined.
9. Those involved in worship ministry are arguably some of the hardest working ____________________ in the entire congregation.
10. We gather to establish the presence of Christ in our ____________________ and region.
11. We want them to see prophetic musicians who are engaged ____________________ in offering their love to Jesus Christ.
12. After services, consider ____________________ with the team.

13. A pastor needs a strong, ____________________ worship leader; a worship leader needs a capable, ____________________ preacher.
14. Respect means we give each other space to make a ____________________.
15. The question isn't whose discernment is right; the question is, are we ____________________ of each other in those moments of decision?
16. So many powerful ministry partnerships have been ____________________ by the adversary because the two didn't talk.
17. Worship leaders have a pastoral heart to help the flock get there, and sometimes songs are not ____________________ the journey needs.
18. Never become a ____________________ for those who are discontent with the pastor.
19. They inspire, break open, support, and ____________________ on their instruments.
20. They were ____________________ and consecrated to their post because they qualified to minister to the Lord.
21. Said another way, we want them to have the ____________________ commandment in ____________________ place.
22. Musicians should be ____________________ to the team.
23. People are often led more strongly by what they ____________________ than what they *hear*.
24. When the screen operator is not fully familiar with the song, they can make a number of ____________________.
25. Musicians, do your leader a favor and ____________________ over at them repeatedly during a song.
26. A worship team should have a list of ____________________ for every person on the worship team.

27. We refuse to become ______________________ when we're asked to adjust our playing.

28. Since worship happens weekly, rehearsing for it should also happen on a

    __________________________ basis.

29. Read meaningful books on worship as a team and ________________________ them.

30. Practice will unify a team musically, but prayer will unify a team ____________________.

FOR GROUP DISCUSSION

1. Choose a couple fill-in-the-blank statements above to talk about in the group.
2. Ask your pastor to come to one of your worship team rehearsals and share with you about the content of this chapter and his or her vision for worship.
3. How strong is our sense of "team"? How strong are our lines of communication? What can we do to strengthen the team dynamics of our worship ministry?
4. How strongly do the team members feel cared for, in their personal walk? Do we share a sense of common vision? Do we pray together as much as we should?

EXPLORING DEEPER

1. Search for three books that will be good for your team to read together over the next year.
2. In what ways do you see "team ministry" in the model of worship leadership that David instituted in his day? Make a note of biblical insights on team ministry that you notice in your studies.

NOTES

CHAPTER TEN

PLANNING THE WORSHIP SERVICE

1. If we go into a worship service with no set list and no rehearsal behind us, it's like going to war without ____________________.
2. Preparation actually empowers ____________________.
3. Love always has an element of ____________________ to it.
4. He'll intentionally make us hesitant and uncertain because He wants us ____________________ extra hard on Him.
5. Self-preparation is a more ____________________ prospect than song preparation.
6. Avoid ____________________ before the service.
7. In the immediacy of the moment, move forward in faith, knowing that the Lord honors ____________________ and directs their hearts.
8. He wants our ____________________, regardless of the songs that are sung.
9. Some worship leaders have the mistaken idea that the solution to any problem in worship is the ____________________ song.
10. Moving away from the set list doesn't necessary guarantee a more ____________________ worship service.
11. It liberates everyone on the worship team to worship freely because we ____________________ where we're going.

12. When you have a boat, you gain the courage to ____.

13. I recommend that worship leaders maintain a ____________________ List of all the songs that are current in their team's repertoire.

14. Expect the Lord to stir interest in your heart when your ____________________ come to the right songs.

15. Plan a set list that foresees a ____________________ in the Spirit.

16. Not every worship service has to have a ____________________.

17. If worship becomes too ____________________, the people will lose interest and disengage.

18. God is full of ____________________, but ruts are comfortably predictable.

19. To get out of a smooth rut sometimes requires something ____________________, even jarring.

20. I encourage worship leaders to intentionally introduce ____________________ and creativity into corporate worship.

21. Who says we have to sing ____________________ in order to worship?

22. Several times the Psalms exhort us to sing to the Lord a *new song*, because He wants our romance to always remain ____________________ and ____________________.

23. New songs force us to ____________________.

24. A new song is a response to something ____________________ God is doing.

25. God wants to give your church its own ____________________.

26. When a song has melodic grab, people will find themselves singing that line ____________________ the day.

FOR GROUP DISCUSSION

1. Choose a couple fill-in-the-blank statements above to talk about in the group.
2. "Preparation actually empowers spontaneity." Have you experienced this to be true? Tell us about your experience.
3. What have you learned about planning extra time into your schedule so you're not in a rushed mode as you enter the meeting?
4. "To get out of a smooth rut sometimes requires something dramatic, even jarring." Do you agree, or is that an exaggeration?
5. Review the author's twelve suggestions under "Keep Worship Fresh," and talk about the ones that interest you most.

EXPLORING DEEPER

1. Put together a Master Song List of the songs that are currently in the repertoire of your local church worship ministry.
2. Plan a way to use Communion in a creative way in an upcoming meeting. Plan the timing, how it will be served, the Scriptures that will be read, and the focus that will be presented. Do the same thing, for another meeting, with the time of offering.
3. Embark on a search for new songs, and find some that you will plan to teach your congregation over the upcoming months.

NOTES

CHAPTER ELEVEN

SONGWRITING

1. Once you know a song, you'll probably remember it for the ____________ of your life.
2. Whenever I'm writing a song, I'm always aware of the potential ____________ of the process before me.
3. It was an incredible feeling to listen to a ____________ of a new song that somehow came out of me.
4. You don't need to be on staff at a church to write worship songs, but I do think you need some of Jesus' ____________ for the church.
5. Something beautiful and releasing happens when believers begin to sing the songs of their own ____________ together.
6. God can find a David in any ____________ place of the earth and carry the songs on the four winds.
7. Each song happens ____________ and differently.
8. The more ____________ songs you write, the better your chances of writing good ones.
9. Something I value about writing with others is that we're all ____________ as writers and humans.
10. Keep collecting your song ideas, no matter how inspired or ____________ they may feel at the time.
11. Find inspiration in your ____________ and journey.

12. A song is proven to be accessible when the ____________________ body of Christ picks it up and sings it enthusiastically.
13. While we want to be authentic and original, bottom line we want you to get our song ____________________ in your head.
14. Learn, therefore, to be ____________________ by allowing others to speak into your work.
15. At the end of the day, just ____________________ is what's going to make you a better songwriter.

FOR GROUP DISCUSSION

1. Choose a couple fill-in-the-blank statements above to talk about in the group.
2. Talk about collaboration in songwriting. Does anyone in the group have experience in this? Could we collaborate in songwriting in our group?
3. What can we do to increase our inspiration in songwriting?
4. Artists take their work personally. In what ways is it positive that we feel so personal about our art? In what ways can it be negative?

EXPLORING DEEPER

1. Find an online link (whether a film or tutorial or written article, etc) on songwriting that you found especially helpful, and share it with everyone in the group.
2. Write three songs of your own, and then share them with someone in the group.

NOTES

CHAPTER TWELVE

HARP & BOWL WORSHIP

1. Based upon this prayer, therefore, we ask for worship on ____________________ as it is in heaven.
2. We've conceived of worship as something that sets the ____________________ for the word of God to be proclaimed.
3. Gazing upon Him is utterly ____________________.
4. This description of heavenly worship is our ____________________ for worship here and now on earth.
5. At its essence is the idea of combining worship and ____________________ as we minister unceasingly before the throne of God.
6. The challenge was ____________________.
7. To be sustainable 24/7, worship must lift our ____________________ to God.
8. In this segment, short ____________________ will often be repeated that focus on the nature of God.
9. We do much singing of Scripture (psalms), and we explore ____________________ song (spiritual songs) every day of the week.
10. Worshipers will latch onto spiritual song best when they realize they can simply repeat ____________________ simple line.
11. We try to keep the spontaneous phrases that are sung simple and ____________________ so that everyone can join in together.

12. The primary way singers develop a passage is by ____________________ a phrase that is then explored.
13. Most were illiterate, and antiphonal singing was used to ____________________ biblical truth.
14. Like John, we must accept the ____________________.

FOR GROUP DISCUSSION

1. Choose a couple fill-in-the-blank statements above to talk about in the group.
2. What is your exposure to or experience with 24/7 worship and intercession? Tell the group about it.
3. In what way should we incorporate harp and bowl into the worship culture of our church?

EXPLORING DEEPER

1. Log onto the live stream of the prayer room at ihopkc.org, and take some time to worship and pray with the live stream. Do you sense the Lord talking to you about 24/7 worship?
2. Study the scriptural connection between worship and intercession. Write down the verses and insights that are especially meaningful to you.

NOTES

CHAPTER THIRTEEN

USING TECHNOLOGY IN WORSHIP

1. Even though the musical expressions of worship teams vary by ________________ and time, the heart behind it all remains true to the original Davidic calling of ministering wholeheartedly to the Lord.
2. Multitracks allow worship teams to supplement their sound with specific synth and rhythmic sounds that are nearly ____________________ to achieve with just the musicians on stage.
3. The wave of the future, however, is on the side of ____________________.
4. Thankfully, though, those who knew better ____________________ brought these instruments into the church.
5. While we've progressed beyond the rock music debate, we face a new one today over things like lighting, video, __________________ instrumental sounds, and more.
6. We worship Jesus, and technology is simply a ____________________ to help.
7. One potential negative is that worshipers can come to ____________________ upon and expect the audio excellence of original recordings in church services.
8. During musical crescendos, it's so easy to rush the timing—but the ______________ cured that for us.
9. Attentive worship leaders are always ready to flow with the ____________________.

10. The track functions like a tutor and helps the musicians become even more

    ______________________.

11. If, on the other hand, we don't master the programs and integration, we'll be constantly thrown off and ______________________ from the things that are truly important.

12. Define what sound you're going for as a team, and ______________________ your resources accordingly.

13. At all costs, strive for unity with your ______________________.

14. It's great to have technology on the team, so add it like you would add another ______________________ to the team.

15. Remind your team to play ______________________ the technology, not over it.

16. ______________________ will hinder the flow of the Spirit and the creative life of your team.

17. Even the ______________________ of learning about the latest technologies are changing.

18. We don't place our dependence upon the *tools* of worship, but keep our eyes centered on the ______________________ of worship—Jesus.

FOR GROUP DISCUSSION

1. Choose a couple fill-in-the-blank statements above to talk about in the group.
2. In what ways might your worship ministry become more effective by using available technologies? Which technologies would you like your church to start using? To stop using?
3. What have you observed to be the benefits and liabilities of technology's usage in worship ministries?

EXPLORING DEEPER

1. Starting with Exodus 36:8, compile several Scriptures that point to the beauty of using creativity in worship.

NOTES

ANSWERS TO CHAPTER QUESTIONS

CHAPTER ONE

1. to commend, applaud, express approval or admiration; to extol in words or in song, to magnify, to glorify
2. raising much to-do about God
3. manifested
4. His
5. His name, His word, His works, His power
6. Who He is
7. He commands it; He loves it; Praise is powerful; Praise is good; He's worthy of it; We were created for this
8. we need to praise Him
9. Man's chief end is to glorify God and enjoy Him forever.
10. When we're up; when we're down; Now; At all times
11. Emotional
12. Around the world; In the congregation; Everywhere we go
13. (your choice of verses)
14. Desire to be held; Token of surrender; To receive from the Lord
15. Lift hands; Clap hands; Play musical instruments; Stand; Kneel; Sing; Speak out; Dance; Shout; In spiritual language
16. the making of a great noise
17. a chair
18. showing respect; it supports alertness, engagement
19. prostration
20. of the humility it requires
21. spiritual release
22. strength
23. "I suppose we dance because we cannot fly."
24. the shout of praise

CHAPTER TWO

1. His omnipresence; His presence where two or three are gathered; the cloud of His glory
2. all we see
3. formula
4. (verse of your choice)
5. (verse of your choice)
6. giving
7. minister to the Lord
8. prepare our hearts through repentance and prayer
9. interest and participation
10. the community; demonic forces; heaven
11. financial; of the heart
12. make
13. dog; reflexively worship
14. a compliment
15. distractions
16. week
17. sacrifice
18. a sacrifice of praise
19. burning
20. costs
21. a true sacrifice of our energy
22. minutes; time

CHAPTER THREE

1. intercessory prayer, the name of Jesus, the confession of God's word, the blood of Christ, and praise
2. gates; hell
3. Man; war
4. Commander-in-Chief
5. mobilize; praise choir
6. vanguard
7. singing; following
8. soldiers; singers
9. how; would
10. prisoners
11. goodness; goodness
12. devil; jailer; greatness
13. chains; delivered
14. shout; praise
15. shout; turn on itself
16. shout
17. rejoice; battle; praise; fights
18. faith
19. power; rejoice
20. naïve; childlike; praise
21. high praise, and the sword of the word
22. high volume; high intensity; high timbre; reflecting the praise around the throne; ascending into the heavens to war on our behalf
23. praises; word
24. high praise; two-edged sword
25. worship; charge
26. praise
27. leading
28. battle
29. release; back off

CHAPTER FOUR

1. (choose any three)
2. musical; heart
3. praises; worshipers
4. humble; exalt
5. worshipers
6. one-way; two-way
7. heard; evident

8. praisers; others
9. gateway
10. one another
11. tragedy; trials
12. Sunday; Monday
13. bottom; losses
14. dreams; affections; best
15. love; learned
16. deep; deep
17. God
18. God
19. Worship Leader
20. successful; Spirit
21. want; good
22. connect; themselves
23. mental
24. perfect; pretense
25. incarnate
26. platform; secret place
27. word
28. soar; truth
29. truth; Spirit
30. hype
31. commandment; place
32. lovers; love
33. sit; hear

CHAPTER FIVE

1. significant
2. perfume; nothing
3. Jesus
4. gift
5. intentionally
6. tears
7. weep
8. hand
9. reproach
10. rules
11. undignified
12. barrenness
13. wholehearted
14. affection
15. examples
16. zeal
17. aura
18. then
19. perfect
20. avoid
21. overcome
22. repentance; despair
23. radiation
24. changing
25. pride
26. presumption
27. performance/audience
28. grooving
29. vehicle
30. controlling

CHAPTER SIX

1. role
2. encounter
3. gaze
4. excellent
5. Lord
6. blessed
7. ourselves
8. enhance
9. analyzer
10. adoring
11. presence
12. earmark
13. power
14. release
15. communication
16. face
17. horizontally
18. strengthen
19. joined
20. ignite
21. teach
22. families
23. profess
24. believers
25. advertising
26. receptivity
27. heart
28. faith
29. changes
30. pace

CHAPTER SEVEN

1. prophecy
2. To move prophetically in worship is to move with an awareness of the desire and leading of the Holy Spirit, moment by moment, to discern the direction of the Spirit, and to help God's people participate in it.
3. key
4. exchange
5. empowers
6. praise; prophecy
7. prophesied
8. broke
9. prophetic
10. prophet
11. called
12. Jesus Himself
13. Scripture
14. human
15. moment
16. rich
17. facelift
18. storm
19. known
20. edifies
21. entire
22. spirit
23. liberty
24. faith
25. learn
26. sing
27. friendship
28. heard

CHAPTER EIGHT

1. appointed
2. leading
3. novice
4. acceptable
5. compatible
6. motivate
7. click tracks
8. tempo
9. tool
10. shore
11. bogged
12. visitors
13. reach
14. public
15. distract

16. invisibility
17. pastors
18. opportunity
19. strive
20. get; lose
21. possibilities
22. difference
23. difficult
24. succinctly
25. horrible
26. connecting
27. culture
28. coffin
29. written
30. disciples

CHAPTER NINE

1. forest fire
2. way
3. support
4. advances
5. motivate
6. pray
7. worshiper
8. participation
9. laborers
10. city
11. spiritually
12. debriefing
13. anointed; anointed
14. mistake
15. considerate
16. splintered
17. everything
18. sounding board
19. prophesy
20. appointed
21. first; first
22. appointed
23. see
24. mistakes
25. look
26. expectations
27. offended
28. weekly
29. discuss
30. spiritually

CHAPTER TEN

1. shoes
2. spontaneity
3. spontaneity
4. leaning
5. rigorous
6. hurrying
7. human leaders
8. hearts
9. right
10. powerful
11. know
12. get out of the boat
13. Master
14. eyes
15. progression
16. theme
17. predictable
18. surprises
19. dramatic
20. variety
21. hymns
22. fresh; adventuresome
23. think
24. new
25. sound
26. throughout

CHAPTER ELEVEN

1. rest
2. power
3. recording
4. zeal
5. journey
6. remote
7. uniquely
8. bad
9. stretched
10. uninspired
11. life
12. wider
13. stuck
14. vulnerable
15. doing it

CHAPTER TWELVE

1. earth
2. atmosphere
3. captivating
4. model
5. intercession
6. sustainability
7. eyes
8. phrases
9. spontaneous
10. one
11. singable
12. isolating
13. teach
14. invitation

CHAPTER THIRTEEN

1. culture
2. impossible
3. technology
4. courageously
5. synthetic
6. tool
7. rely
8. clicks
9. unexpected
10. creative
11. distracted
12. budget
13. lead pastor
14. member
15. with
16. Smugness
17. channels
18. object